Abhinav Bindra

"I was just trying to concentrate on shooting," he said. "I wasn't thinking of making history..." These are the words of India's great shooter – Abhinav Bindra. Concentration is the key word of this Olympic gold medallist. Like Arjuna of Mahabharata he concentrated on his aim and achieved it. True to his name 'Abhinav' which means 'new' he has set a new record in the history of India. After a long wait of 28 years, India scored a gold medal. It was India's first individual gold medal at the Olympics. Indian national anthem played at the Beijing Olympics in 2008, after a long span of years – it was last played when the men's field hockey team of India won the gold medals at the Moscow Olympics in 1980.

Abhinavas a child

His full name is Abhinav Singh Bindra. He belongs to an affluent Sikh Khatri family of Punjab living in Zirakpur, Mohali. His father Dr. Apjit Singh Bindra and mother Babli Bindra are businessmen. They promote Hitech Group of companies that has interests in agro and dog-food-processing, computer gaming, livestock genetics and pharmaceuticals. It has a huge turnover.

During school days

Abhinav was born in Dehradun on September 28, 1982. He did his schooling from Doon School, Dehradun and St. Stephens School, Chandigarh. He pursued higher studies at the University of Colorado and was awarded degree of Bachelors in Business Administration (BBA) from there. He holds a Diploma in Sports Mental Management from Munich and Lanny School of Mental Management, USA. He is pursuing Doctorate in Masters of Business Management. On September 8, 2008, he was conferred Honorary Doctorate in Literature from SRM University, Chennai.

From a very young age he had a passion for shooting. His affluent father encouraged him and installed an indoor shooting range in the backyard of their home in Patiala, in Punjab. He started taking part in shooting at the age of twelve and won in 1995, the Ropar Shooting Championship. The next year, that is in 1996, when he was thirteen, he won six gold medals at Punjab State Shooting Championship, in senior and junior categories. He also broke the junior world record. Since it was not an international event this breaking of the record went unrecognised. In 1997, Abhinav made his presence felt by breaking the national record twice. The next year he became the national champion in both the senior and the junior categories. He re-established the national record. Once he

After winning the prestigious Olympic gold medal with his parents

Coach and mentor Dr. Bhattacharya with Abhinav Bindra

had established a name in the nationals, Abhinav was ready for the international events.

At the tender age of fifteen Abhinav became a shooter and participated at the Kuala Lumpur Commonwealth Games held in 1998, where he was the youngest participant. He broke the world record in

Training in England

1999 in junior men event. He won the gold medal in SAF Games and re-established a World record as Senior and Junior National Champion and at the same time set a new national record. In 2000, he represented the country in the world shooting championship in Barcelona. At Sydney Olympics in 2000, he was the youngest Indian athlete and youngest shooter. In 2001, at the Munich World Cup he made a junior world record by scoring 597/600 and won a bronze. He had created a world record in this event. After this he shot into limelight. In 2001, Abhinav won six gold medals at various international meets in European Circuit. He won a gold in the Manchester Commonwealth Games in 2002, when he competed in Air rifle event in the Pairs and silver in the Individual event. Abhinav Bindra had made his mark and all the eyes were now focused on this shooting star.

At Athens Olympics in 2004, Abhinav broke the Olympic record, but did not win a medal. Though, he was the third he was below 100 points that dropped his position to the seventh. This was very disappointing for him. However in July 2006, he became the first Indian shooter to win gold in World Championship in Zagreb. Previously in 1962 Dr. Karni Singh had won a silver medal. The same year (2006), Abhinav Bindra won the gold medal in Pairs event and bronze in the Singles event in Melbourne Commonwealth Games. However, he could not attend the Asian Games at Doha in 2006, owing to a back injury.

The achievements of Abhinav are consistently improving. What goes behind the scenes has to be seen. Abhinav thrives on pressure, like all champions. According to him it is as essential as air and water. But it has to be in right measure. Too much or too less is bad. It is absolutely necessary to bring out the best in a performer. This is

Competing at 2010 Commonwealth Games

realized by his coach who has been putting pressure on Abhinav to perform better consistently.

Besides the pressure that he faces time and again there is good measure of training involved. Abhinav is tireless where training is concerned. For him training is life. He works for eight hours a day. He is always attempting different targets and stimulations that are very tough.

Abhinav has the best indoor shooting range which his father has provided. Here he trains alone which in itself is very tough though at the same time advantageous. The electronic targets at his personal shooting range gives him the freedom and advantage to practice for hours at an end without being disturbed and helps him improve his style and shot. Others, who are not in his position, have to be content at aiming at paper targets in camps provided from time to time.

Ecstatic on winning the Olympic gold medal

Receiving Arjun Award from the then President of India Sh. K.R. Narayanan (2000)

For him training is like food. He practices diligently. Before the Olympics he took tough commando training in Germany for three weeks. Thirty five lakhs were given to him by the National Sports Development Funds for his three month training in Germany. This money took care of his trainer's fee as well as of the sports psychologist.

Lt. Col Dhillon was his first coach. Dr. Amit Bhatacharjee is his mental coach. Both have been closely associated with him since the beginning of his career as a shooter. In fact they were the ones who spotted his potential very early in his life. His present coach is Gabriele Buhlmann from Basel, Switzerland. He trained Abhinav in Germany before the Olympics. He is a very tough trainer and has left no stone

Ace shooter Abhinav with Smt. Sonia Gandhi after winning Olympic gold medal at Bejing

unturned in giving a rigorous training. This he could provide for he was himself a shooter and no ordinary shooter but one who was five-time shooter at the Olympics. What more could Abhinav desire. Gabriele's coaching and Abhinav's diligence bore fruit when he won the Olympic gold for India.

His coaches are constantly helping him perform consistently.

Abhinav Bindra's father has spent enormous amount of money on his training and has given the best support to his son. The senior Bindra has requested the government to provide training in Germany for 45 days at a stretch, three times a year. This has been approved and sanctioned by the government.

However, the Bindras on their part have not spared anything to provide the best for Abhinav. Lanny Bassham has been engaged by them to help Abhinav build mental toughness. Bassham is a former Olympic champion and two-time world champion. He has devised a mental management system. This he created after interviewing many Olympic champions. The gist of his study is that one should not bow down or avoid pressure but use it for ones ends. In his book 'With Winning in Mind' he has written "To Abhinav, future Olympic Champion" before autographing the book. This is exactly what Abhinav does. He works with the pressure, under pressure to achieve through using pressure.

Besides mental training and training as an ace marksman, Abhinav has to keep his body fit. He does jogging and stretching exercises as a daily routine to keep physically fit. He is completely dedicated in mind and body to the sport he loves and pursues as a career. Shooting is a different kind of sport. It requires complete dedication in terms of stamina and concentration. Other athletes have to pay attention to bodily fitness, but a shooter has to have

President of India Smt. Pratibha Patil presenting the Padma Bhushan award to Abhinav Bindra (2009)

Totally immersed in concentration during practice

control of the mind and at the same time total body fitness with which to compete. They need a different kind of stamina that involves mind and body. On top of it, they need concentration. These three things have to be in the right measure to achieve a good shot. A flicker of the eye or a slight distraction can cause one to miss the target. He knows that one has to have a synchronicity of mind, eye and finger to pull the trigger at the right time and hit the target.

The shooter has to not only look after himself, but have full knowledge and control of the instrument he uses. Here it is the rifle. He has to check that his rifle is in perfect order. A slight disorder and the trigger happy shooter could land in a problem. Abhinav is well aware of this and takes great care of his rifles.

In India very few sportsperson are talented, intelligent and hard workers as Abhinav. He has been lucky to have parents who appreciated his talent and provided infrastructure for the potential to be nurtured. Providing him with his own shooting range and mental and physical

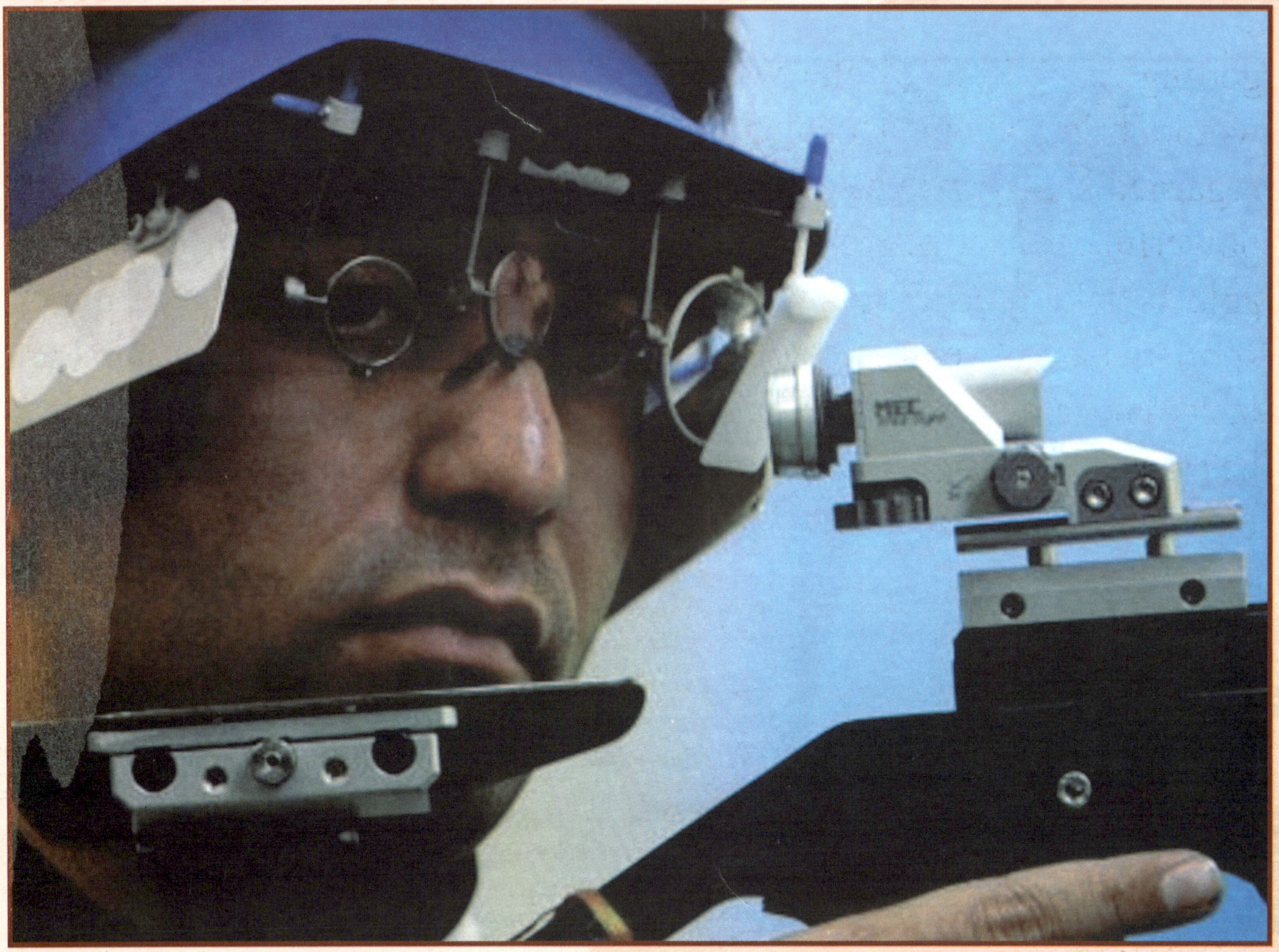

Participating in 10 metres Air Rifle Competition

coach was just the beginning in their effort to see that he blossomed and grew to be a great shooter. They have left nothing to chance. Every aspect of his training has been meticulously taken care. Whether physical or mental, nothing has been overlooked. This is the reason why when he won the Olympic gold medal he said that he owed the gold medal to his parents, family and the coaches.

In India, there is too much emphasis on cricket. Other sports are either completely ignored or neglected. After winning the gold medal and getting recognised by the world as a great shooter, Abhinav hopes it would bring about a change in sports arena. Shooting is generally regarded an expensive sport here, which only the affluent, talented and powerful can aspire to pursue as a career. Therefore, only a few have been able to take it as a sport and that too for a short time. Most of the sportsperson have not been able to sustain their pursuit in this sport for lack of infrastructure and encouragement. Owing to this reason, shooting has been relegated to a secondary position by sports enthusiasts in India. People like Abhinav Bindra could sustain this sport for long and achieve

Receiving honorary rank of Lt Colonel in the Territorial Army

something because of the facilities that they have. He has an air-conditioned shooting range which has a totally computerised Target Transportation System of International standard.

Cabinet Minister Shri Ramvilas Paswan presenting plague and cheque of Rs. 15 lacs to Abhinav Bindra (2008)

However, thanks to Abhinav and the Olympic gold medal he won India has woken. More and more sports persons have shown interest for this sport and have opted for this sport as a profession. The government too has started showing interest in this erstwhile neglected sport. The National Rifle Association has uplifted the standard of shooting as a sport. They have helped the Indian shooters get international exposure and polish their skills. Thanks to the Indian shooters, the concept of sports has changed.

Abhinav Bindra has received many awards because of his excellent performance in shooting, besides the medals that he has won. In 2000, he received the Arjun Award from the Indian government. In 2001, he was

Chief Justice of Mumbai High Court Mr. Chandra Shekar Dharmadhikari felicitating Abhinav

given the Rajiv Gandhi Khel Ratna, which is India's highest sports award. He was given the Padma Bhushan, which is one of the most prestigious civilian awards of India.

Besides this he was given some cash rewards. The Punjab State government gave a cash reward of rupees 1 crore. The Haryana State Government and BCCI each rewarded 25 lakhs, while the Steel Ministry of India awarded 15 lakh rupees. The Railway Ministry of India has entitled him a free lifetime railway pass.

Ace shooter Abhinav Bindra waving the Indian Flag

Abhinav Bindra is the CEO of Abhinav Futuristics, the sole agent of German-made Walther weapons in India. He is also running a sports trust aimed at churning future champions in India. He is sponsored by Samsung and Sahara Group.

Abhinav remains focused, a quality that a shooter requires.

□□□